4D

AN AUGMENTED REALITY
SCIENCE EXPERIENCE

CURIOUS PEARL
SCIENCE GIRL

CURIOUS PEARL
IDENTIFIES THE REASON
FOR SEASONS

by Eric Braun

illustrated by Stephanie Dehennin

PICTURE WINDOW BOOKS
a capstone imprint

Curious Pearl here! Do you like science? I sure do! I have all sorts of fun tools to help me observe and investigate, but my favorite tool is my science notebook. That's where I write down questions and facts that help me learn more about science. Would you like to join me on my science adventures? You're in for a special surprise!

Download the Capstone 4D app!

Videos for all of the sidebars in this book are at your fingertips with the 4D app.

To download the Capstone 4D app:

- Search in the Apple App Store or Google Play for "Capstone 4D"
- Click Install (Android) or Get, then Install (Apple)
- Open the application
- Scan any page with this icon

You can also access the additional resources on the web at www.capstone4D.com using the password

pearl.seasons

Some kids are into sports. Other kids know all about dogs or trains. Not me. I love science! Lately, I have been studying sunsets. Today, my friend Sal and I swam in the lake. Later, we watched the sunset. It was beautiful. I wrote down the time in my science notebook.

Sunset Times:
Tuesday: 7:39
Wednesday: 7:38
Thursday: 7:37
Friday: 7:35
Saturday: 7:34

"The Sun is setting earlier every day," Sal said.

"That's because the season is changing," I said. "Summer is almost over. Fall will be here soon, and then winter."

"I get it," Sal said. "In summer we have long days. But during winter, days are short." Sal thought for a second and then grinned. "We better get ready for snow," he said.

"Not yet!" I said.

"Remember my pen pal, Mateo, from Argentina?" asked Sal. "Well, he said they got snow today. I bet it's headed our way."

"Wow," I said. I shivered in my swimsuit. "I do NOT want snow today!"

"We better go change into some warm clothes," joked Sal.

"Don't worry," I said. "We won't get snow tonight." I shivered again. "But we do need to head to my place. Let's go!"

We went to my apartment. Sal dug out some winter clothes. My dad helped me find a website that shows temperatures all over the world. We found Mateo's city in Argentina. Argentina is in the Southern Hemisphere. We live in the Northern Hemisphere.

Next we looked for Mateo's city on the globe.

Sal pointed to Argentina on the globe. "So, is it winter in the Southern Hemisphere right now?"

"Eureka! Yes, it is!" I said. Eureka is a scientific word. I use it when I get excited about a new discovery.

I jotted down some notes in my notebook.

Seasons in the Northern and Southern Hemispheres happen at opposite times. When it's summer in the Northern Hemisphere, it's winter in the Southern Hemisphere.

"Let's think," I said. "What makes it warm on Earth?"

"The Sun," replied Sal.

"Eureka! That's true!" I said. "And it says here that Earth has an axis. It's an imaginary pole that runs from top to bottom through Earth's center."

"That makes sense," said Sal.

← Earth's axis

"Earth spins, or rotates, on its axis. It moves around, or orbits, the Sun at the same time," I said. "It's amazing we all aren't dizzy!" joked Sal.

Earth rotates once in 24 hours. That's why a day on Earth is 24 hours.

"Let's try something," I said to Sal as I walked over to the globe in the corner. I grabbed a small lamp and removed its shade.

"Let's say this lamp is the Sun," I said.

The lamp shined a bright warm spot on the top half of the globe. "That half is the Northern Hemisphere," I said. "The light shining on the bottom half, or the Southern Hemisphere, is slanted. It's not as strong."

Northern Hemisphere

Southern Hemisphere

"Right," said Sal.

"As Earth rotates, part of it is pointed toward the Sun. The other part of Earth is pointed away from the Sun," I told Sal.

"But that doesn't explain why weather changes," said Sal, "or why snow is coming."

"Snow isn't coming!" I said.

While Earth rotates, part of it is pointed directly at the Sun. That part of Earth experiences daytime. The part of Earth pointed away from the Sun is in darkness. It is nighttime there.

I spun the globe around again. "Because of Earth's tilt, the Northern Hemisphere is getting sunshine longer than the Southern Hemisphere. That means the day is shorter in the south."

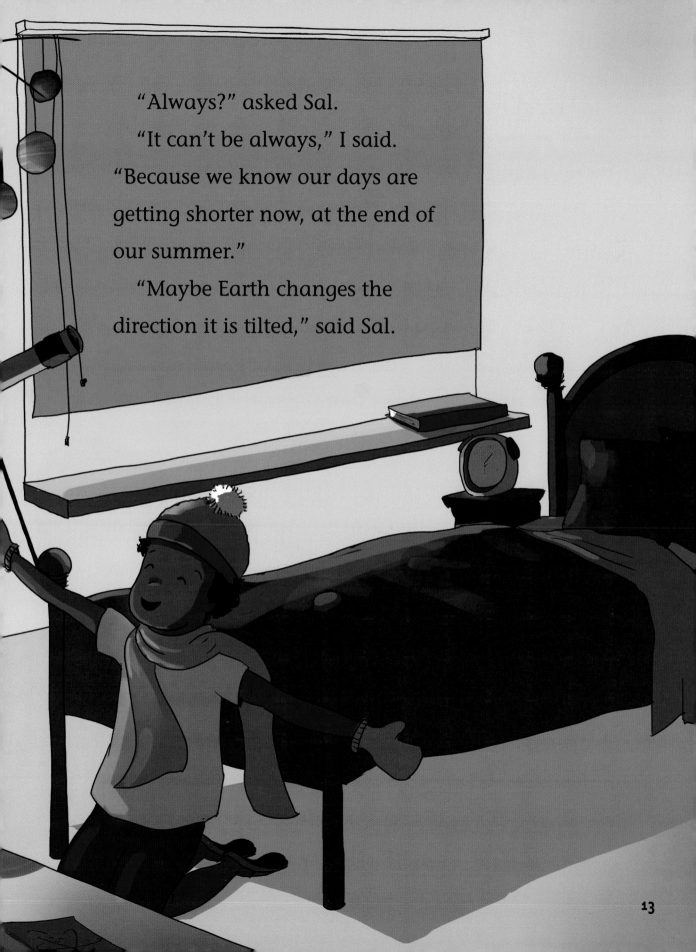

"Always?" asked Sal.

"It can't be always," I said.
"Because we know our days are
getting shorter now, at the end of
our summer."

"Maybe Earth changes the
direction it is tilted," said Sal.

Dad sat down and joined us. "Earth's axis is always tilted in the same direction," he said.

"So how does the weather change?" I asked.

"Remember, Earth also moves around the Sun," he said. "In fact, it takes one year for it to go around the Sun one time."

"Eureka! That's right!" I cheered.

"I get it," Sal said. "It's winter in the top half of Earth when more light is shining on the bottom half."

I picked up the globe and walked around the lamp. Soon, more of its light was shining on the top half of the globe.

"And it's summer in the top half when Earth is over here," I said. "Now more light is shining on the Northern Hemisphere."

Seasonal changes happen because of Earth's tilt on its axis and its orbit around the Sun.

15

I moved the globe around the lamp to see how the light changed. "Areas near the equator get lots of sunlight all year," I said. "As Earth orbits the Sun, the amount of sunlight doesn't change much there. The weather doesn't change much either."

"Okay, but what about areas near Earth's top and bottom?" asked Sal.

"You mean the North and South Poles?" I replied. "Near the poles, the amount of sunlight changes a lot. The North Pole gets six months of sunlight during summer. The South Pole is in darkness that whole time. In winter, the North Pole is in darkness for about 11 weeks straight."

"That's a big difference!" Sal said.

"Yes, it is!" I said. "Let me write this down."

Places near Earth's equator receive a lot of sunlight. So areas near the equator don't have as many seasonal changes as areas farther away from the equator.

North
Pole

Equator

South Pole

Dad's phone rang, so he walked out of the room. Sal grabbed a jacket and put it on. But soon his face was getting red. He must have been getting sweaty in his hat, gloves, and jacket. He said, "So Earth moves around the Sun one time every year. It's always the same."

"Yes, and we can predict when the seasons will change," I said.

"I predict it will not snow tonight," Sal said.

"I predict you are right!" I replied.

The change in seasons affects people, plants, and animals. Farmers know the best time to grow different crops. Some animals, like many snakes, hibernate during winter. Some animals migrate, or move to different areas, to find food or shelter.

The next afternoon, Sal and I went swimming in the lake again. Later we looked at my science notebook. Sal guessed the Sun would set at 7:33 p.m. He was right!

"Still no snow," I said.

"Thank goodness!" Sal said. "I'm going for another swim. Will you take my picture? I want to e-mail it to Mateo. He won't believe I'm swimming in the middle of his snowstorm!"

Tuesday: 7:39
Wednesday: 7:38
Thursday: 7:37
Friday: 7:35
Saturday: 7:34
Sunday: ??

When and where does the Sun rise?

Earth orbits the Sun. As it does, daylight changes with the seasons. Get up before sunrise one morning to learn how daylight changes in your area. Don't forget to bring a pad of paper and a pencil.

1. With an adult, find an open area like a beach or large field. Write down what time the Sun rises. Take notes about what you see*. Draw the eastern and western horizons. Put a mark to show where the Sun rose.

2. That night, go to the same place to see the sunset. Take notes again about what you see. Put a mark on your diagram showing exactly where the Sun went down.

3. Repeat the activity about three months later. In your notes, write about any changes you notice. Why do you think there were changes?

*Be careful not to look directly at the Sun.

GLOSSARY

equator—an imaginary line around the middle of Earth; it divides the Northern and Southern Hemispheres

eureka—a cry of joy or satisfaction

hibernate—to spend winter in a deep sleep; animals hibernate to survive low temperatures and a lack of food

Northern Hemisphere—the half of Earth's land and water surfaces that are north of the equator

North Pole—the northern-most point on Earth; the North Pole is in the Arctic

orbit—to travel around an object in space; an orbit is also the path an object follows while circling an object in space

predict—to say what you think will happen in the future

Southern Hemisphere—the half of Earth's land and water surfaces that are south of the equator

South Pole—the southernmost point on Earth; the South Pole is in Antarctica

temperature—a measure of how hot or cold something is

READ MORE

Algarra, Alejandro and Rocio Bonilla. *What Causes Weather and Seasons?* New York: Barron's Educational Series, Inc., 2016.

Berne, Emma Carlson. *The Secrets of Earth.* Smithsonian: Planets. Mankato, Minn.: Capstone Press, 2016.

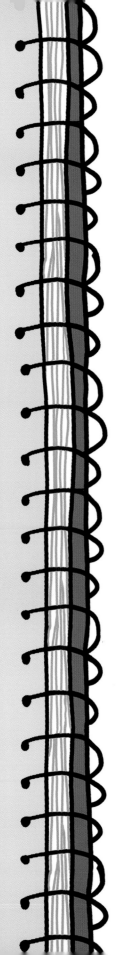

INTERNET SITES

Use FactHound to find Internet sites related to this book.

Visit *www.facthound.com*

Just type in 9781515813439 and go.

CRITICAL THINKING QUESTIONS

How would life on Earth be different if the planet was not tilted?

The Sun gives us light and heat. How do changes in light and heat affect plants and animals?

Because we know about Earth's tilt and orbit, we can predict when seasons will change. How might this be helpful? What would happen if seasons changed without warning?

MORE BOOKS IN THE SERIES

INDEX

Thanks to our adviser for his expertise,
research, and advice:
Christopher T. Ruhland, PhD
Professor of Biological Sciences
Department of Biology
Minnesota State University, Mankato

Editor: Shelly Lyons
Designer: Ted Williams
Art Director: Nathan Gassman
Production Specialist: Katy LaVigne
The illustrations in this book were digitally
produced.

Picture Window Books are published by
Capstone, 1710 Roe Crest Drive, North Mankato,
Minnesota 56003
www.mycapstone.com

**Library of Congress Cataloging-in-
Publication Data**
Cataloging-in-Publication information is on file
with Library of Congress.
Names: Braun, Eric, author. | Dehennin,
Stephanie, illustrator.
Title: Curious Pearl Identifies the Reason for
Seasons: 4D An Augmented Reality Science
Experience
ISBN 978-1-5158-1343-9 (library binding)
ISBN 978-1-5158-1347-7 (paperback)
ISBN 978-1-5158-1359-0 (eBook PDF)

Printed and bound in the USA.
010373F17